Contents

Introduction

The theme of Life and Death has passed through the ages and has awakened the minds and thoughts of both some of the greatest philosophers and the common man. This topic is as vast as it is unimaginable. The meaning of life and the meaning of death have been central to philosophy, literature, psychology, biology and many other sciences. The fight for life and the battle against death is one of the original ones. The clash of good and evil, light and darkness, life and death has been described throughout the ages by both the most exquisite writers and the greatest philosophers. To this day, this theme awakens both our admiration and our fears - the fear of the unknown, our archaic fears of annihilation and destruction. At the same time, it is the person who gives life and very often takes life. This is a phenomenon that has echoed through the centuries, to this day.

In this book, I have tried to gather the thoughts and words of great philosophers from antiquity to the present day, great writers, and even movie and book characters. This book is for every waking mind who seeks the answers to the eternal questions, seeks meaning, seeks and discovers himself, both in his experience and in the experience of many before him. Like you, I seek Life every day, and one day at the end of my search, I will find his best friend, Death.

About the author

Valentin Boyadzhiev is a trained nutritionist, graduated Master of Psychology in "Psychology and Psychopathology of Development". He has acquired Professional Qualification "Teacher of Psychology" and Postgraduate Professional Qualification "Psychological Counseling in Psychosomatic and Social Adaptation Disorders". He has obtained a Psychoanalysis Diploma and he has specialized in Psychoanalytic Psychotherapy. He is a member of the Association "Bulgarian Psychoanalytic Space", "International Society of Applied Psychoanalysis" and „International Alliance of Holistic Therapists". He is a lecturer on issues related to nutrition, diet, supplementation, food and sports. He is also a teacher and a lecturer in the field of psychology, logic, ethics, law, and philosophy. He has been a school psychologist since 2017. He has been participating annually in scientific conferences on psychology, psychotherapy, dietetics and medicine. His main interest and practice are in the field of psychoanalysis and clinical psychology.

Quotes about life and death

A man with outward courage dares to die;
a man with inner courage dares to live.
Lao Tzu

A normal human being does not want the
Kingdom of Heaven: he wants life on
earth to continue.
George Orwell

A single death is a tragedy; a million
deaths is a statistic.
Joseph Stalin

A word is dead when it is said, some say. I
say it just begins to live that day.
Emily Dickinson

Above all, I have been a sentient being, a
thinking animal, on this beautiful planet,

and that in itself has been an enormous
privilege and adventure.
Oliver Sacks

Ψ

Absolute silence leads to sadness. It is the
image of death.
Jean-Jacques Rousseau

Ψ

After all, to the well-organized mind,
death is but the next great adventure.
J K Rowling

Ψ

After your death, you will be what you
were before your birth.
Arthur Schopenhauer

Ψ

All good is hard. All evil is easy. Dying,
losing, cheating, and mediocrity is easy.

Stay away from easy.
Scott Alexander

Ψ

All men think that all men are mortal but
themselves.
Edward Young

Ψ

All your sorrows have been wasted on
you if you have not yet learned how to be
wretched.
Seneca

Ψ

Ancient Egyptians believed that upon
death they would be asked two questions
and their answers would determine
whether they could continue their
journey in the afterlife. The first question
was, 'Did you bring joy?' The second was,
'Did you find joy?
Leo Buscaglia

And as long as you're subject to birth and death, you'll never attain enlightenment.
Bodhidharma

And I will show that nothing can happen more beautiful than death.
Walt Whitman

And so we will believe in our even a hundred times more worthy of their attention.
Friedrich Nietzsche

Ψ

And we wept that one so lovely should have a life so brief.
William Cullen Bryant

Ψ

Anything I've done that was ultimately
worthwhile initially scared me to death.
Betty Bender

Ψ

As a well spent day brings happy sleep, so
life well used brings happy death.
Leonardo da Vinci

Ψ

As soon as you'll realize that it was a gift,
you'll be free.
Maxime Lagacé

Ψ

Be ashamed to die until you have won
some victory for humanity.
Horace Mann

Ψ

Be sure the safest rule is that we should
not dare to live in any scene in which we
dare not die. But, once realise what the

true object is in life — that it is not pleasure, not knowledge, not even fame itself, 'that last infirmity of noble minds' — but that it is the development of character, the rising to a higher, nobler, purer standard, the building-up of the perfect Man — and then, so long as we feel that this is going on, and will (we trust) go on for evermore, death has for us no terror; it is not a shadow, but a light; not an end, but a beginning!
Lewis Carroll

Ψ

Because I have loved life, I shall have no sorrow to die.
Amelia Burr

Ψ

Because life is fragile and death inevitable, we must make the most of each day.
Thomas S. Monson

Ψ

Because there is no glory in illness. There
is no meaning to it.
John Green

Ψ

Birth and death are the most singular
events we experience – and the
contemplation of death, as of birth,
should be a thing of beauty, not
ignobility.
Jacob K. Javits

Ψ

Birth and death; we all move between
these two unknowns.
Bryant H. McGill

Ψ

Birth is not a beginning; death is not an
end. There is existence without
limitation; there is continuity without a

starting point.
Zhuangzi

By becoming deeply aware of our mortality, we intensify our experience of every aspect of life.
Robert Greene

Carve your name on hearts, not tombstones. A legacy is etched into the minds of others and the stories they share about you.
Shannon L. Alder

Cowards die many times before their deaths; The valiant never taste of death but once.
William Shakespeare (Julius Caesar)

Crying does not indicate that you are weak. Since birth, it has always been a sign that you are alive.
Charlotte Bronte

Death – the last sleep? No, it is the final awakening.
Walter Scott

Death anxiety is greater in those who feel they have lived an unfulfilled life.
Irvin Yalom

Death comes to all, but great achievements build a monument which shall endure until the sun grows cold.
Ralph Waldo Emerson

Death commences too early – almost before you're half-acquainted with life – you meet the other.
Tennessee Williams

Death destroys a man: the idea of Death saves him.
E.M. Forster

Death ends a life, not a relationship.
Mitch Albom

Death in itself is nothing; but we fear to be we know not what, we know not where.
John Dryden

Death is a challenge. It tells us not to waste time... It tells us to tell each other

right now that we love each other.
Leo Buscaglia

Ψ

Death is a distant rumor to the young.
Andrew A. Rooney

Ψ

Death is a law, not a punishment.
Jean Dubos

Ψ

Death is a stripping away of all that is not you. The secret of life is to "die before you die" – and find that there is no death.
Eckhart Tolle

Ψ

Death is a word, and it is the word, the image, that creates fear.
Jiddu Krishnamurti

Ψ

Death is as sure for that which is born, as
birth for that which is dead. Therefore
grieve not for what is inevitable.
Bhagavad Gita

Death is beautiful when seen to be a law,
and not an accident.
Henry David Thoreau

Death is but a door, time is but a window.
I'll be back!
Ghostbusters II

Death is life's high meed.
John Keats

Death is like a mirror in which the true
meaning of life is reflected.
Sogyal Rinpoche

Ψ

Death is more universal than life;
everyone dies but not everyone lives.
Andrew Sachs

Ψ

Death is nature's way of saying, "Your
table is ready".
Robin Williams

Ψ

Death is never an apology.
Soul King

Ψ

Death is no more than passing from one
room into another. But there's a
difference for me, you know. Because in
that other room I shall be able to see.
**Helen Keller (Remember that Helen Keller
was blind)**

Ψ

Death is not extinguishing the light; it is only putting out the lamp because the dawn has come.
Rabindranath Tagore

Ψ

Death is not something you get over. It's the rip that exposes life in a before and after chasm, and all you can do is try to exist as best you can in the after.
Lily Graham

Ψ

Death is not the biggest fear we have; our biggest fear is taking the risk to be alive – the risk to be alive and express what we really are.
Miguel Angel Ruiz

Death is not the greatest loss in life. The greatest loss is what dies inside us while we live.
Norman Cousins

Death is not the opposite of life, but a part of it.
Haruki Murakami

Death is nothing else but going home to God, the bond of love will be unbroken for all eternity.
Mother Teresa

Death is nothing, but to live defeated is to die every day.
Napoleon Bonaparte

Death is only the end if you assume the story is about you.
Welcome to Night Vale (Podcast)

Death is our friend precisely because it brings us into absolute and passionate presence with all that is here, that is natural, that is love...
Rainer Maria Rilke

Death is so terribly final, while life is full of possibilities.
George R.R. Martin (Game of Thrones)

Death is the destination we all share. No one has ever escaped it. And that is as it should be because death is very likely the single best invention of life. It is life's change agent, it clears out the old to

make way for the new.
Steve Jobs

Ψ

Death is the greatest illusion of all.
Osho

Ψ

Death is the ultimate boundary of human matters.
Horace

Ψ

Death is the veil which those who live call life; They sleep, and it is lifted.
Percy Bysshe Shelley

Ψ

Death makes equal the high and low.
John Heywood

Ψ

Death may be the greatest of all human blessings.
Socrates

Ψ

Death must be so beautiful. To lie in the soft brown earth, with the grasses waving above one's head, and listen to silence. To have no yesterday, and no to-morrow. To forget time, to forgive life, to be at peace.
Oscar Wilde

Ψ

Death must be so beautiful. To lie in the soft brown earth, with the grasses waving above one's head, and listen to silence. To have no yesterday, and no to-morrow. To forget time, to forget life, to be at peace.
Oscar Wilde

Ψ

Death never takes the wise man by
surprise, he is always ready to go.
Jean de La Fontaine

Death pays all debts.
William Shakespeare

Death smiles at us all, all a man can do is
smile back.
Marcus Aurelius

Death takes no bribes.
Benjamin Franklin

Death will never make sense to your
mind. Only time and self-understanding
will alleviate your suffering.
Maxime Lagacé

Ψ

Death? Be as proud as you want: bore me later, because Love is sovereign here. Life never ends. Joy comes in the morning. Glory hallelujah. And let it be so.
Anne Lamott

Ψ

Deep into that darkness peering, long I stood there, wondering, fearing, doubting, dreaming dreams no mortal ever dared to dream before.
Edgar Allan Poe

Ψ

Die happily and look forward to taking up a new and better form. Like the sun, only when you set in the west can you rise in the east.
Rumi

Ψ

Do not fear death so much but rather the inadequate life.
Bertolt Brecht

Ψ

Do not fear death. Death is always at our side. When we show fear, it jumps at us faster than light. But, if we do not show fear, it casts its eye upon us gently and then guides us into infinity.
Laughing Bull

Ψ

Do not seek death. But do not fear it either. There cannot be life without death, it is inescapable.
Keisei Tagami

Ψ

Do not seek death. Death will find you. But seek the road which makes death a fulfillment.
Dag Hammarskjold

Ψ

Do you not know that a man is not dead
while his name is still spoken?
Terry Pratchett

Ψ

Do you see the gift that you had? Do you
see how lucky you were?
Maxime Lagacé

Ψ

Don't be afraid to cry. It will free your
mind of sorrowful thoughts.
Hopi (Native American)

Ψ

Dream as if you'll live forever, live as if
you'll die today.
James Dean

Dying is a very dull, dreary affair. And my advice to you is to have nothing whatever to do with it.
W. Somerset Maugham

Dying is an art.
Sylvia Plath

Dying is easy; it's living that's difficult.
Frederick Lenz

Dying is like coming to the end of a long novel – you only regret it if the ride was enjoyable and left you wanting more.
Jerome P. Crabb

Each day, we wake slightly altered, and the person we were yesterday is dead. So why, one could say, be afraid of death,

when death comes all the time?
John Updike

Each night, when I go to sleep, I die. And the next morning, when I wake up, I am reborn.
Mahatma Gandhi

Ψ

Earth has no sorrow that heaven cannot heal.
Thomas Moore

Ψ

End? No, the journey doesn't end here. Death is just another path, one that we all must take. The grey rain-curtain of this world rolls back, and all turns to silver glass, and then you see it.
J.R.R. Tolkien

Ψ

Endings are not always bad. Most times they're just beginnings in disguise.
Kim Harrison

Enjoy life. There's plenty of time to be dead.
Hans Christian Andersen

Even death is not to be feared by one who has lived wisely.
Buddha

Even trees do not die without a groan.
Henry David Thoreau

Every exit is an entry somewhere else.
Tom Stoppard

Every man must do two things alone; he must do his own believing and his own dying.
Martin Luther

Ψ

Every man's life ends the same way. It is only the details of how he lived and how he died that distinguish one man from another.
Ernest Hemingway

Ψ

Everybody wants to go to heaven, but nobody wants to die.
Unknown

Ψ

Everybody's gotta die sometime. That's life.
Archie Bunker

Ψ

Everyone dies but not everyone lives.
William Wallace

Everyone dies eventually, whether they have power or not. That's why you need to think about what you'll accomplish while you're alive.
Mary Macbeth

Everyone dies. But not everyone really lives.
Unknown

Everyone wants to be foremost in this future-and yet death and the stillness of death are the only things certain and common to all in this future!
Friedrich Nietzsche

Everything is ridiculous if one thinks of
death.
Thomas Bernhard

For after all, the best thing one can do
when it is raining is let it rain.
Henry Wadsworth Longfellow

For life and death are one, even as the
river and the sea are one.
Khalil Gibran

For life be, after all, only a waitin' for
somethin' else than what we're doin'; and
death be all that we can rightly depend
on.
Bram Stoker (Dracula)

For some moments in life there are no
words.
David Seltzer

For what is it to die but to stand naked in
the wind and to melt into the sun? And
when the earth shall claim your limbs,
then shall you truly dance.
Kahlil Gibran

From my rotting body, flowers shall grow
and I am in them and that is eternity.
Thomas Moore

Give me liberty or give me death.
Patrick Henry

Give place to others, as others have given
place to you. Equality is the soul of

equity. Who can complain of being comprehended in the same destiny, wherein all are involved?
Michel de Montaigne

God conceals from men the happiness of death that they may endure life.
Marcus Annaeus Lucanus

God pours life into death and death into life without a drop being spilled.
Unknown

Good men must die, but death cannot kill their names.
Unknown

Ψ

Goodbyes are only for those who love with their eyes. Because for those who

love with heart and soul there is no such
thing as separation.
Rumi

Grief and love are conjoined, you don't
get one without the other. All I can do is
love her, and love the world, emulate her
by living with daring and spirit and joy.
Jandy Nelson

Grief is forever. It doesn't go away; it
becomes a part of you, step for step,
breath for breath.
Jandy Nelson

Grief turns out to be a place none of us
know until we reach it.
Joan Didion

Grief, when it comes, is nothing like we
expect it to be.
Joan Didion

Grieving is not weakness nor absence of
faith. Grieving is as natural as crying
when you are hurt, sleeping when you
are tired or sneezing when your nose
itches. It is nature's way of healing a
broken heart.
Doug Manning

Guilt is perhaps the most painful
companion to death.
Elisabeth Kubler-Ross

Happiness can exist only in acceptance.
George Orwell

He is terribly afraid of dying because he hasn't yet lived.
Franz Kafka

Ψ

He who is not busy being born is busy dying.
Bob Dylan

Ψ

Here is the test to find whether your mission on Earth is finished: if you're alive, it isn't.
Richard Bach

Ψ

Hold infinity in the palm of your hand.
William Blake

Ψ

How can the dead be truly dead when they still live in the souls of those who

are left behind?
Carson McCullers

How lucky I am to have something that
makes saying goodbye so hard.
Winnie The Pooh

How strange that this sole thing that is
certain and common to all, exercises
almost no influence on men, and that
they are the furthest from regarding
themselves as the brotherhood of death!
Friedrich Nietzsche

How strange that this sole thing that is
certain and common to all, exercises
almost no influence on men, and that
they are the furthest from regarding
themselves as the brotherhood of death!

I am ready to meet my Maker. Whether
my Maker is prepared for the great
ordeal of meeting me is another matter.
Winston Churchill

I believe that fear of life brings a greater
fear of death.
David Blaine

Ψ

I believe that imagination is stronger
than knowledge – myth is more potent
than history – dreams are more powerful
than facts – hope always triumphs over
experience – laughter is the cure for grief
– love is stronger than death.
Robert Fulghum

Ψ

I cannot pretend I am without fear. But
my predominant feeling is one of
gratitude.
Oliver Sacks

Ψ

I carry death in my left pocket.
Sometimes I take it out and talk to it:
"Hello, baby, how you doing? When you

coming for me? I'll be ready".
Charles Bukowski

I could just remember how my father
used to say that the reason for living was
to get ready to stay dead a long time.
William Faulkner

I despise wisdom and the blessings of this
world. It is all worthless, fleeting,
illusory, and deceptive, like a mirage.
Anton Chekhov

I discovered to my joy, that it is life, not
death, that has no limits.
Gabriel García Márquez

I do not believe that any man fears to be
dead, but only the stroke of death.
Francis Bacon

I do not fear death. I had been dead for
billions and billions of years before I was
born, and had not suffered the slightest
inconvenience from it.
Mark Twain

I don't believe in an afterlife, so I don't
have to spend my whole life fearing hell,
or fearing heaven even more. For
whatever the tortures of hell, I think the
boredom of heaven would be even worse.
Isaac Asimov

Ψ

I don't like paradise, as they probably
don't have obsessions there.
Alda Merini

Ψ

I don't want to die without any scars.
Chuck Palahniuk

Ψ

I feel monotony and death to be almost
the same.
Charlotte Brontë

Ψ

I have always imagined that paradise will
be a kind of library.
J.K. Rowling

Ψ

I have had an intercourse with the world,
the special intercourse of writers and
readers.
Olivier Sacks

Ψ

I have loved and been loved; I have been
given much and I have given something
in return; I have read and traveled and
thought and written.
Olivier Sacks

Ψ

I have noticed that even those who assert
that everything is predestined and that
we can change nothing about it still look
both ways before they cross the street.
Stephen Hawking

Ψ

I have wrestled with death. It is the most
unexciting contest you can imagine. It
takes place in an impalpable greyness,
with nothing underfoot, with nothing
around, without spectators, without
clamour, without glory, without the great
desire of victory, without the great fear
of defeat, in a sickly atmosphere of tepid
skepticism, without much belief in your

own right, and still less in that of your
adversary.
Joseph Conrad

I love those who can smile in trouble,
who can gather strength from distress,
and grow brave by reflection. 'Tis the
business of little minds to shrink, but
they whose heart is firm, and whose
conscience approves their conduct, will
pursue their principles unto death.
Leonardo da Vinci

I regard the brain as a computer which
will stop working when its components
fail. There is no heaven or afterlife for
broken down computers; that is a fairy
story for people afraid of the dark.
Stephen Hawking

I regret not death. I am going to meet my
friends in another world.
Ludovico Ariosto

I shall not die of a cold. I shall die of
having lived.
Willa Cather

I think death is equally terrible for
everyone. Young people, old people, the
good, the bad; it's always the same. It's
rather fair in its treatment. There's no
such thing as a terrible death, that's why
it's frightening.
Sunako

I want to be all used up when I die.
George Bernard Shaw

I wanted a perfect ending. Now I've learned, the hard way, that some poems don't rhyme, and some stories don't have a clear beginning, middle, and end. Life is about not knowing, having to change, taking the moment and making the best of it, without knowing what's going to happen next. Delicious ambiguity.
Gilda Radner

I went to the woods because I wished to live deliberately, to front only the essential facts of life, and see if I could not learn what it had to teach, and not, when I came to die, discover that I had not lived.
Henry David Thoreau

I will never stop grieving Bailey because I will never stop loving her. That's just how

it is.
Jandy Nelson

I would fain do something to make the idea of life to us to be more than friends in the sense of that sublime possibility.
Friedrich Nietzsche

I would love to believe that when I die I will live again, that some thinking, feeling, remembering part of me will continue. But as much as I want to believe that, and despite the ancient and worldwide cultural traditions that assert an afterlife, I know of nothing to suggest that it is more than wishful thinking.
Carl Sagan

I would rather die a meaningful death
than to live a meaningless life.
Corazon Aquino

I'm not afraid of death because I don't
believe in it. It's just getting out of one
car, and into another.
John Lennon

I'm not afraid to die, I just don't want to
be there when it happens.
Woody Allen

I'm the one that's got to die when it's
time for me to die, so let me live my life
the way I want to.
Jimi Hendrix

If a man can bridge the gap between life
and death, if he can live on after he's
dead, then maybe he was a great man.
James Dean

If I can see pain in your eyes, then share
with me your tears. If I can see joy in
your eyes, then share with me your smile.
Santosh Kalwar

If life must not be taken too seriously,
then so neither must death.
Samuel Butler

If my doctor told me I had only six
minutes to live, I wouldn't brood. I'd type
a little faster.
Isaac Asimov

If one was to think constantly of death,
the business of life would stand still.
Samuel Johnson

If there are no dogs in Heaven, then when
I die I want to go where they went.
Will Rogers

If we can prove an afterlife, then we have
less pressure to make our physical life
last forever.
Chuck Palahniuk

If we don't know life, how can we know
death?
Confucius

If we lose love and self respect for each other, this is how we finally die.
Maya Angelou

Ψ

If you are mindful of death, it will not come as a surprise-you will not be anxious. You will feel that death is merely like changing clothes. Consequently, at that point you will be able to maintain your calmness of mind.
Dalai Lama

Ψ

If you gave someone your heart and they died, did they take it with them? Did you spend the rest of forever with a hole inside you that couldn't be filled?
Jodi Picoult

Ψ

If you have a sister and she dies, do you stop saying you have one? Or are you

always a sister, even when the other half
of the equation is gone?
Jodi Picoult

If you make every game a life and death
proposition, you're going to have
problems. For one thing, you'll be dead a
lot.
Dean Smith

If you're not ready to die for it, take the
word "freedom" out of your vocabulary.
Malcolm X

In all the relations of life and death, we
are met by the color line.
Frederick Douglass

In my end is my beginning.
Mary, Queen of Scots

In the end one needs more courage to live
than to kill himself.
Albert Camus

In the short term, you'll see a
thunderstorm. Once the thunderstorm is
over, you'll see flowers.
Maxime Lagacé

Isn't it sad that so often it takes facing
death to appreciate life and each other
fully?
Esther Earl

It is as natural to die as it is to be born.
Francis Bacon

Ψ

It is foolish and wrong to mourn the men
who died. Rather we should thank God
that such men lived.
George S. Patton

Ψ

It is human to have your soul brought to
a crisis you did not anticipate.
The Dune Series

Ψ

It is necessary to be strong in the face of
death, because death is intrinsic to life. It
is for this reason that I tell my students:
aim to be the person at your father's
funeral that everyone, in their grief and
misery, can rely on. There's a worthy and
noble ambition: strength in the face of
adversity.
Jordan Peterson (12 Rules for Life)

It is not death that a man should fear, but
he should fear never beginning to live.
Marcus Aelius Aurelius

Ψ

It is not length of life, but depth of life.
Ralph Waldo Emerson

Ψ

It is nothing to die. It is frightful not to
live.
Victor Hugo

Ψ

It is said that your life flashes before your
eyes just before you die. That is true, it's
called Life.
Terry Pratchett

It is the fate — the genetic and neural fate — of every human being to be a unique individual, to find his own path, to live his own life, to die his own death.
Oliver Sacks

It is the secret of the world that all things subsist and do not die, but retire a little from sight and afterwards return again.
Ralph Waldo Emerson

It is the unknown we fear when we look upon death and darkness, nothing more.
J.K. Rowling (Harry Potter)

It makes me happy to see that men do not want to think at all of the idea of death!
Friedrich Nietzsche

It matters not how a man dies, but how he lives. The act of dying is not of importance, it lasts so short a time.
Samuel Johnson

Ψ

It seems to me that if you or I must choose between two courses of thought or action, we should remember our dying and try so to live that our death brings no pleasure to the world.
John Steinbeck

Ψ

It will stay in your head first, and then in your heart. Those places will always be reserved.
Maxime Lagacé

Ψ

It's matters not how a man dies, but how he lives.
Samuel Johnson

Ψ

It's a positive way to keep their spirit
alive in the world, by keeping it alive in
yourself.
Patrick Swayze

Ψ

It's better to burn out than to fade away.
Neil Young

Ψ

It's only when we truly know and
understand that we have a limited time
on earth – and that we have no way of
knowing when our time is up – that we
will begin to live each day to the fullest,
as if it was the only one we had.
Elisabeth Kubler-Ross

Ψ

Let children walk with Nature, let them
see the beautiful blendings and

communions of death and life, their
joyous inseparable unity, as taught in
woods and meadows, plains and
mountains and streams of our blessed
star, and they will learn that death is
stingless indeed, and as beautiful as life.
John Muir

Let life be beautiful like summer flowers
and death like autumn leaves.
Rabindranath Tagore

Let thy hope of heaven master thy fear of
death.
William Gurnall

Let us endeavor so to live that when we
come to die even the undertaker will be
sorry.
Mark Twain

Ψ

Let us not pray to be sheltered from dangers but to be fearless when facing them.
Rabindranath Tagore

Ψ

Let us so live that when we come to die even the undertaker will be sorry.
Mark Twain

Ψ

Life and death are balanced on the edge of a razor.
Homer

Ψ

Life and death are illusions. We are in a constant state of transformation.
Alejandro Gonzalez Inarritu

Life and death are one thread, the same
line viewed from different sides.
Lao Tzu

Life and death. At some point we're
gonna leave this world. Do I know when
Absolutely not.
Terrell Owens

Life and death. They are somehow
sweetly and beautifully mixed, but I don't
know how.
Gloria Swanson

Life asked death; "Why do people love
me, but hate you " Death responded,
"Because you are a beautiful lie, and I am
the painful truth.
Unknown

Life does not cease to be funny when people die any more than it ceases to be serious when people laugh.
George Bernard Shaw

Life doesn't imitate art, it imitates bad television.
Woody Allen

Life has more meaning in the face of death.
Robert Greene

ψ

Life is a series of natural and spontaneous changes. Don't resist them; that only creates sorrow. Let reality be reality. Let things flow naturally forward in

whatever way they like.
Lao Tzu

Ψ

Life is but a dream for the dead.
Gerard Way

Ψ

Life is eternal, and love is immortal,Life is
eternal, and love is immortal, and death
is only a horizon; and a horizon is
nothing save the limit of our sight.
Rossiter Worthington Raymond

Ψ

Life is for the living. Death is for the dead.
Let life be like music. And death a note
unsaid.
Langston Hughes

Ψ

Life is hard. After all, it kills you.
Katharine Hepburn

Life is like a very short visit to a toy shop
between birth and death.
Desmond Morris

Life is pleasant. Death is peaceful. It's the
transition that's troublesome.
Isaac Asimov

Ψ

Life is rather a state of embryo, a
preparation for life; a man is not
completely born till he has passed
through death.
Benjamin Franklin

Ψ

Life is so beautiful that death has fallen in
love with it, a jealous, possessive love
that grabs at what it can. But life leaps
over oblivion lightly, losing only a thing

or two of no importance, and gloom is just a passing shadow of a cloud.
Yann Martel (Life of Pi)

Life isn't fair, nor should you expect it to be. No matter how well you prepare, shit will happen, often when you least expect it.
Ed Latimore

Ψ

Life should not be a journey to the grave with the intention of arriving safely in a pretty and well preserved body, but rather to skid in broadside in a cloud of smoke, thoroughly used up, totally worn out, and loudly proclaiming "Wow! What a Ride!
Hunter S. Thompson

Ψ

Life was such a fragile thing?as delicate
and as beautiful as a butterfly, as
ephemeral as a sunset. Death is peaceful.
Death is quiet, silent. It is calming.
Akanksha

Life will undertake to separate us, and we
must each set off in search of our own
path, our own destiny or our own way of
facing death.
Paulo Coelho

Life without an ideal is spiritual death.
Emma Goldman

Ψ

Live as if you were to die tomorrow.
Learn as if you were to live forever.
Mahatma Gandhi

Ψ

Live how we can, yet die we must.
William Shakespeare

Ψ

Live or die, but don't poison everything.
Anne Sexton

Ψ

Live your life that the fear of death can
never enter your heart.
Tecumseh

Ψ

Live your life, do your work, then take
your hat.
Henry David Thoreau

Ψ

Long after her death I felt her thoughts
floating through mine.
Vladimir Nabokov (Lolita)

Ψ

Losing your life is not the worst thing
that can happen. The worst thing is to
lose your reason for living.
Jo Nesbø

Love never dies a natural death. It dies
because we don't know how to replenish
its source. It dies of blindness and errors
and betrayals. It dies of illness and
wounds; it dies of weariness, of
witherings, of tarnishings.
Anais Nin

Man alone chimes the hour. And, because
of this, man alone suffers a paralyzing
fear that no other creature endures. A
fear of time running out.
Mitch Albom

Man always thinks about the past before
he dies, as if he were frantically searching
for proof that he truly lived.
Jet Black

Man cannot possess anything as long as
he fears death. But to him who does not
fear it, everything belongs.
Leo Tolstoy

Many of us crucify ourselves between two
thieves – regret for the past and fear of
the future.
Fulton Oursler

Many people die at twenty-five and aren't
buried until they are seventy-five.
Benjamin Franklin

Maybe all one can do is hope to end up
with the right regrets.
Arthur Miller

Memory and forgetfulness are as life and
death to one another. To live is to
remember and to remember is to live. To
die is to forget and to forget is to die.
Samuel Butler

Men are never really willing to die except
for the sake of freedom: therefore they do
not believe in dying completely.
Albert Camus

Mostly it is loss which teaches us about
the worth of things.
Arthur Schopenhauer

My happiness grows in direct proportion
to my acceptance, and in inverse
proportion to my expectations.
Michael J. Fox

My mama always used to tell me: 'If you
can't find somethin' to live for, you best
find somethin' to die for'.
Tupac Shakur

My sister will die over and over again for
the rest of my life.
Jandy Nelson

Neither fire nor wind, birth nor death can
erase our good deeds.
Buddha

Neither the sun, nor death can be looked
at steadily.
François de La Rochefoucauld

Ψ

No art is possible without a dance with
death.
Kurt Vonnegut

Ψ

No one ever told me that grief felt so
much like fear.
C.S. Lewis

Ψ

No one here gets out alive.
Jim Morrison

Ψ

No one is actually dead until the ripples
they cause in the world die away.
Terry Pratchett

Ψ

No one really knows why they are alive
until they know what they'd die for.
Martin Luther King Jr

Ψ

No truth can cure the sorrow we feel
from losing a loved one. No truth, no
sincerity, no strength, no kindness can
cure that sorrow. All we can do is see it
through to the end and learn something
from it, but what we learn will be no help
in facing the next sorrow that comes to
us without warning.
Haruki Murakami

Ψ

Nothing is ever certain.
Alice Sebold

Ψ

Now, of all the benefits that virtue confers upon us, the contempt of death is one of the greatest, as the means that accommodates human life with a soft and easy tranquillity, and gives us a pure and pleasant taste of living, without which all other pleasure would be extinct.
Michel de Montaigne

Of course you don't die. Nobody dies. Death doesn't exist. You only reach a new level of vision, a new realm of consciousness, a new unknown world.
Henry Miller

Once you accept your own death, all of a sudden you're free to live. You no longer care about your reputation. You no longer care except so far as your life can be used tactically to promote a cause you

believe in.
Saul Alinsky

Ψ

One cannot get through life without pain... What we can do is choose how to use the pain life presents to us.
Bernie S. Siegel

Ψ

One lives in the hope of becoming a memory.
Antonio Porchia

Ψ

One regret dear world, that I am determined not to have when I am lying on my deathbed is that I did not kiss you enough.
Hafiz of Persia

Ψ

One should die proudly when it is no
longer possible to live proudly.
Friedrich Nietzsche

Only people who are capable of loving
strongly can also suffer great sorrow, but
this same necessity of loving serves to
counteract their grief and heals them.
Leo Tolstoy

Only to live, to live and live! Life,
whatever it may be!
Fyodor Dostoevsky

Our culture's zeal for longevity reveals
our incredible collective fear of death.
Ram Dass

Our dead are never dead to us, until we
have forgotten them.
George Eliot

Our death is not an end if we can live on
in our children and the younger
generation. For they are us; our bodies
are only wilted leaves on the tree of life.
Albert Einstein

Ψ

Our life and death are the same thing.
When we realize this fact we have no fear
of death anymore, and we have no actual
difficulty in our life.
Shunryu Suzuki

Ψ

Parting is all we know of heaven, and all
we need of hell.
Emily Dickinson

Ψ

People die all the time. Life is a lot more fragile than we think. So you should treat others in a way that leaves no regrets. Fairly, and if possible, sincerely. It's too easy not to make the effort, then weep and wring your hands after the person dies.

Haruki Murakami

Ψ

People do not die for us immediately, but remain bathed in a sort of aura of life which bears no relation to true immortality but through which they continue to occupy our thoughts in the same way as when they were alive. It is as though they were traveling abroad.

Marcel Proust

People living deeply have no fear of
death.
Anais Nin

Preparing for death is one of the most
empowering things you can do. Thinking
about death clarifies your life.
Candy Chang

Religion is the human response to being
alive and having to die.
Forrest Church

She was no longer wrestling with the
grief, but could sit down with it as a
lasting companion and make it a sharer
in her thoughts.
George Eliot

Since we're all going to die, it's obvious
that when and how don't matter.
Albert Camus

Ψ

Sing your death song, and die like a hero
going home.
Tecumseh

Ψ

Some people are so afraid to die that they
never begin to live.
Henry Van Dyke

Ψ

Success is failure recycled. Life is death
reborn.
Jonathan Lockwood Huie

Ψ

Take nothing for granted. Keep in mind
that it can come at anytime. Even today.
Maxime Lagacé

Ψ

Tell your friend that in his death, a part of you dies and goes with him. Wherever he goes, you also go. He will not be alone.
Jiddu Krishnamurti

Ψ

That it will never come again is what makes life so sweet.
Emily Dickinson

Ψ

That's what literature is. It's the people who went before us, tapping out messages from the past, from beyond the grave, trying to tell us about life and death! Listen to them!
Connie Willis

Ψ

The anguish of death hangs over and leads the human spirit to wonder about

the mysteries of existence, man's destiny,
life, the world.
E. Morin

Ψ

The best way to get praise is to die.
Italian Proverb

Ψ

The bitterest tears shed over graves are
for words left unsaid and deeds left
undone.
Harriet Beecher Stowe

Ψ

The boundaries which divide Life from
Death are at best shadowy and vague.
Who shall say where the one ends, and
where the other begins?
Edgar Allan Poe

Ψ

The certainty of death and the
uncertainty of the hour of death is a
source of grief throughout our life.
E. Morin

The day which we fear as our last is but
the birthday of eternity.
Seneca

The dead can survive as part of the lives
of those that still live.
Kenzaburō Ōe

The death of a beloved is an amputation.
C.S. Lewis

The fear of death follows from the fear of
life. A man who lives fully is prepared to

die at any time.
Mark Twain

Ψ

The fear of death is the beginning of
slavery.
Robert Anton Wilson

Ψ

The fear of death is the most unjustified
of all fears, for there's no risk of accident
for someone who's dead.
Albert Einstein

Ψ

The first breath is the beginning of death.
Thomas Fuller

Ψ

The first step toward change is
awareness. The second step is acceptance.
Nathaniel Branden

$$\Psi$$

The funny thing about facing imminent death is that it really snaps everything else into perspective.
James Patterson

$$\Psi$$

The goal of all life is death.
Sigmund Freud

$$\Psi$$

The harder the pain, the longer the path to recovery, the better the opportunity to learn.
Maxime Lagacé

$$\Psi$$

The hardest thing you overcome are the ones that give the most meaning.
Maxime Lagacé

$$\Psi$$

The highest tribute to the dead is not
grief but gratitude.
Thornton Wilder

The hour of departure has arrived, and
we go our separate ways, I to die, and you
to live. Which of these two is better only
God knows.
Socrates

The idea is to die young as late as
possible.
Ashley Montagu

The idea of a good society is something
you do not need a religion and eternal
punishment to buttress; you need a
religion if you are terrified of death.
Gore Vidal

Ψ

The last enemy that shall be destroyed is death.
J.K. Rowling

Ψ

The life of the dead is placed in the memory of the living.
Marcus Tullius Cicero

Ψ

The man who lives without conflict, who lives with beauty and love, is not frightened of death because to love is to die.
Jiddu Krishnamurti

Ψ

The meaning of life is that it stops.
Franz Kafka

Ψ

The more you know who you are, and
what you want, the less you let things
upset you.
Stephanie Perkins

The most important thing to arrive on
your deathbed satisfied and grateful is to
first live your life fully.
Maxime Lagacé

The ones that love us never really leave
us.
Sirius Black (Harry Potter)

The only real ending is death. Everything
else is a transition.
Robert Greene

The only thing I know is everything you love will die. The first time you meet someone special, you can count on them one day being dead and in the ground.
Chuck Palahniuk

The opposite of love is not hate, it's indifference. The opposite of art is not ugliness, it's indifference. The opposite of faith is not heresy, it's indifference. And the opposite of life is not death, it's indifference.
Elie Wiesel

The people we most love do become a physical part of us, ingrained in our synapses, in the pathways where memories are created.
Meghan O'Rourke

The phoenix must burn to emerge.
Janet Fitch

Ψ

The real question is not whether life exists after death. The real question is whether you are alive before death.
Osho Rajneesh

Ψ

The real question of life after death isn't whether or not it exists, but even if it does what problem this really solves.
Ludwig Wittgenstein

Ψ

The reports of my death are greatly exaggerated.
Mark Twain

Ψ

The source of sorrows lies not in leaving life, but in leaving that which gives it

meaning.
Raymond Radiguet

The strongest intimidation, by the way, is
the invention of a hereafter with a hell
everlasting.
Friedrich Nietzsche

The trouble with life in the fast lane is
that you get to the other end in an awful
hurry.
John Jensen

The typical human behaviour is to seek
security and certainty. We fear death
because it's the unknown and nobody can
give us answers.
Maxime Lagacé

The world would be dramatically better if everyone had to experience a near death event growing up. Everyone will instantly value their time more, and be happier.
ChuchuTrain

There are far, far better things ahead than any we leave behind.
C.S. Lewis

There are only three things that can kill a farmer: lightning, rolling over in a tractor, and old age.
Bill Bryson

There is a sacredness in tears. They are not the mark of weakness, but of power. They speak more eloquently than ten thousand tongues. They are the messengers of overwhelming grief, of

deep contrition, and of unspeakable love.
Washington Irving

Ψ

There is an afterlife. I am convinced of
this.
Paulo Coelho

Ψ

There is love in holding and there is love
in letting go.
Elizabeth Berg

Ψ

There is no birth, there is no death; there
is no coming, there is no going; there is
no same, there is no different; there is no
permanent self, there is no annihilation.
We only think there is.
Thich Nhat Hahn

Ψ

There is no conclusive evidence of life after death, but there is no evidence of any sort against it. Soon enough you will know, so why fret about it?
Robert A. Heinlein

There is no cure for birth and death save to enjoy the interval.
George Santayana

There is no death. Only a change of worlds.
Chief Seattle (Native American)

There is no grief like the grief that does not speak.
Henry Wadsworth Longfellow

There is no pause in life, the moment we
pause, we stop living.
Lailah Gifty Akita

There is only one god and his name is
Death, and there is only one thing we say
to Death: 'Not today'.
Syrio Forel (Games Of Thrones)

These births and deaths are changes in
nature which we are mistaking for
changes in us.
Swami Vivekananda

They are not dead who live in the hearts
they leave behind.
Tuscarora (Native American)

They say you die twice. One time when you stop breathing and a second time, a bit later on, when somebody says your name for the last time.
Banksy

Ψ

Things we lose have a way of coming back to us in the end, if not always in the way we expect.
J.K. Rowling

Ψ

This aspect of reality, this weird scary aspect of life, can just wreck everything if you don't figure out at some point that it is what makes life so profound, meaningful, rich, complex, wild.
Anne Lamott

Ψ

Those men who, in war, seek to preserve their lives at any rate commonly die with

shame and ignominy, while those who
look upon death as common to all, and
unavoidable, and are only solicitous to
die with honour, oftener arrive at old age
and, while they live, live happier.
Xenophon

Though death be poor, it ends a mortal
woe.
William Shakespeare

To be fully alive, fully human, and
completely awake is to be continually
thrown out of the nest. To live fully is to
be always in no-man's-land, to
experience each moment as completely
new and fresh. To live is to be willing to
die over and over again.
Pema Chödrön

To die laughing must be the most
glorious of all glorious deaths!
Edgar Allan Poe

Ψ

To die will be an awfully big adventure.
Peter Pan

Ψ

To fear death is nothing other than to
think oneself wise when one is not. For it
is to think one knows what one does not
know. No one knows whether death may
not even turn out to be the greatest
blessings of human beings. And yet
people fear it as if they knew for certain
it is the greatest evil.
Socrates

Ψ

To live in hearts we leave behind is not to
die.
Thomas Campbell

Ψ

To lose a brother is to lose someone with whom you can share the experience of growing old, who is supposed to bring you a sister-in-law and nieces and nephews, creatures who people the tree of your life and give it new branches.
Yann Martel (Life of Pi)

Ψ

To lose your father is to lose the one whose guidance and help you seek, who supports you like a tree trunk supports its branches.
Yann Martel (Life of Pi)

Ψ

To the well-organized mind, death is but the next great adventure.
J.K. Rowling

Ψ

Too many people are thinking of security instead of opportunity. They seem to be more afraid of life than death.
James F. Byrnes

Too weird to live, too rare to die!
Hunter S. Thompson

Try as much as possible to be wholly alive with all your might, and when you laugh, laugh like hell. And when you get angry, get good and angry. Try to be alive. You will be dead soon enough.
William Saroyan

Unable are the loved to die for love is immortality.
Emily Dickinson

Unbeing dead isn't being alive.
E.E. Cummings

We all die. The goal isn't to live forever, the goal is to create something that will.
Chuck Palahniuk

We are all alone, born alone, die alone, and—in spite of True Romance magazines — we shall all someday look back on our lives and see that, in spite of our company, we were alone the whole way.
Hunter S. Thompson

Ψ

We are born from a quiet sleep, and we die to a calm awakening.
Zhuangzi

Ψ

We must constantly remind ourselves
that we are eternity, infinite, beyond
birth and death.
Frederick Lenz

Ψ

We owe respect to the living; to the dead
we owe only truth.
Voltaire

Ψ

We should always, as near as we can, be
booted and spurred, and ready to go, and,
above all things, take care, at that time,
to have no business with any one but
one's self. Why for so short a life tease
ourselves with so many projects?
Michel de Montaigne

Ψ

We sometimes congratulate ourselves at
the moment of waking from a troubled
dream; it may be so the moment after

death.
Nathaniel Hawthorne

Ψ

We trouble our life by thoughts about death, and our death by thoughts about life.
Michel de Montaigne

Ψ

What is called a reason for living is also an excellent reason for dying.
Albert Camus

Ψ

What is history? Its beginning is that of the centuries of systematic work devoted to the solution of the enigma of death, so that death itself may eventually be overcome. That is why people write symphonies, and why they discover mathematical infinity and

electromagnetic waves.
Boris Pasternak

What we have once enjoyed deeply we can never lose. All that we love deeply becomes a part of us.
Helen Keller

What would life be worth if there were no death? Who would enjoy the sun if it never rained? Who would yearn for the day if there were no night?
Glenn Ringtved

Whatever you want to do, do it now. There are only so many tomorrows.
Michael Landon

When a person is born we rejoice, and when they're married we jubilate, but when they die we try to pretend nothing has happened.
Margaret Mead

Ψ

When confronted with two alternatives, life and death, one is to choose death without hesitation.
Yamamoto Tsunetomo

Ψ

When death overtakes us, all that we have is left to others; all that we are we take with us.
Unknown

Ψ

When he shall die, take him and cut him out in little stars, and he will make the face of heaven so fine that all the world will be in love with night and pay no

worship to the garish sun.
William Shakespeare (Romeo and Juliet)

Ψ

When I shall die, let it be doing that I had designed.
Ovid

Ψ

When it's time to die, let us not discover that we have never lived.
Henry David Thoreau

Ψ

When people don't express themselves, they die one piece at a time.
Laurie Halse Anderson

Ψ

When someone we love dies, we get so busy mourning what died that we ignore what didn't.
Ram Dass

Ψ

When those you love die, the best you can do is honor their spirit for as long as you live.
Patrick Swayze

Ψ

When we are learning the world, we know things we cannot say how we know. When we are relearning the world in the aftermath of a loss, we feel things we had almost forgotten, old things, beneath the seat of reason.
Meghan O'Rourke

Ψ

When we finally know we are dying, and all other sentient beings are dying with us, we start to have a burning, almost heartbreaking sense of the fragility and preciousness of each moment and each being, and from this can grow a deep,

clear, limitless compassion for all beings.
Sogyal Rinpoche

Ψ

Where is it I've read that someone
condemned to death says or thinks, an
hour before his death, that if he had to
live on some high rock, on such a narrow
ledge that he'd only room to stand, and
the ocean, everlasting darkness,
everlasting solitude, everlasting tempest
around him, if he had to remain standing
on a square yard of space all his life, a
thousand years, eternity, it were better to
live so than to die at once.
Fyodor Dostoevsky

Ψ

Whether or not there's an afterlife, screw
it. Just live your life right here, right now
before it's too late.
Maxime Lagacé

Ψ

While I thought that I was learning how
to live, I have been learning how to die.
Leonardo da Vinci

Ψ

Who would endure life if it were not for
the hope of death?
L.M. Montgomery

Ψ

Why should I fear death? If I am, death is
not. If death is, I am not. Why should I
fear that which cannot exist when I do?
Epicurus

Ψ

Without birth and death, and without the
perpetual transmutation of all the forms
of life, the world would be static, rhythm-
less, undancing, mummified.
Alan Watts

ψ

Yea, all things live forever, though at times they sleep and are forgotten.
H. Rider Haggard

ψ

You are dead – what am I speaking to?
Philip Pullman

ψ

You are facing death and danger and competition, but at any moment, you can decide to have a fearless mindset.
Robert Greene

ψ

You attend the funeral, you bid the dead farewell. You grieve. Then you continue with your life. And at times the fact of her absence will hit you like a blow to the chest, and you will weep. But this will happen less and less as time goes on. She

is dead. You are alive. So live.
Neil Gaiman

Ψ

You can grieve all your life, but what's
the point? You still have your life. Don't
waste it.
Maxime Lagacé

Ψ

You die in the middle of your life, in the
middle of a sentence.
John Green

Ψ

You know, what's so dreadful about dying
is that you are completely on your own.
Vladimir Nabokov (Lolita)

Ψ

You make a commitment that you're
going to take whatever lesson that person
or animal was trying to teach you, and

you make it true in your own life.
Patrick Swayze

Ψ

You may be proud, wise, and fine, but
death will wipe you off the face of the
earth as though you were no more than
mice burrowing under the floor, and your
posterity, your history, your immortal
geniuses will burn or freeze together
with the earthly globe.
Anton Chekhov

Ψ

You needn't die happy when your time
comes, but you must die satisfied, for you
have lived your life from the beginning to
the end.
Stephen King

Ψ

You want to live – but do you know how
to live? You are scared of dying – and, tell

me, is the kind of life you lead really any
different from being dead?
Seneca

You'll drift apart, it's true, but you'll be
out in the open, part of everything alive
again.
Philip Pullman

Final Words

I am happy that this book reaches every reader around the world. I have included in it all those thoughts, reflections and words of the great ones that impressed and inspired me. I hope you found something useful and inspiring, too. Thank you for being a part of the wonderful world of this wonderful science, namely philosophy. See you soon! Best regards, Valentin Boyadzhiev.